First
Facts®

ANCIENT EGYPT

MUMMIES

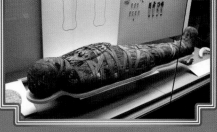

BY KREMENA SPENGLER

Consultant:
Leo Depuydt
Professor, Department of Egyptology
and Ancient Western Asian Studies
Brown University,
Providence, Rhode Island

Capstone

Mankato, Minnesota

First Facts are published by Capstone Press,
151 Good Counsel Drive, P.O. Box 669, Mankato, Minnesota 56002.
www.capstonepress.com

Library of Congress Cataloging-in-Publication Data
Spengler, Kremena.
    Mummies / by Kremena Spengler.
      p. cm. — (First facts. Ancient Egypt)
      Summary: "Describes mummies in ancient Egypt, including how and why people were
mummified" — Provided by publisher.
      Includes bibliographical references and index.
      ISBN-13: 978-1-4296-1916-5 (hardcover)
      ISBN-10: 1-4296-1916-3 (hardcover)
      1. Mummies — Egypt — Juvenile literature. I. Title. II. Series.
DT62.M7S66 2009
932 — dc22   2007050646

Editorial Credits
Jennifer Besel, editor; Alison Thiele, designer; Wanda Winch, photo researcher;
    Marcy Morin, page 21 project production

Photo Credits
Capstone Press/Karon Dubke, 21; Getty Images Inc./AFP, 11; Getty Images Inc./AFP/Ben Curtis, 14–15; Getty
Images Inc./AFP/Cris Bouroncle, 20; Getty Images Inc./Roger Viollet/Boyer, 16; Getty Images Inc./
Patrick Landmann, cover, 17; The Image Works/Topham/Werner Forman Archive/E. Strouhal Location: 101, 10;
Shutterstock/Antonio Petrone, 9 (right), 18–19; Shutterstock/Juriah Mosin, 1; Shutterstock/Juriah Mosin, 9
(left); Shutterstock/YKh, background throughout; SuperStock, Inc./age fotostock, 13 (left); SuperStock, Inc./
Image Asset Management Ltd., 13 (right); UNICORN Stock Photos/Jean Higgins, 6–7; Wood Ronsaville
Harlin, Inc./Matthew Frey, 4

Essential content terms are bold and are defined at the bottom of the page where they first appear.

072010
5843VMI

TABLE OF CONTENTS

PRESERVING THE DEAD

Imagine pulling a dead person's brain out the nose with a hook. Now picture replacing the person's insides with rags. Ancient Egyptians did these things. They wanted to keep dead bodies from rotting. It's a process called **mummification**.

mummification: the process of keeping a dead body from rotting

ANCIENT EGYPT

The time in history called ancient Egypt began around 3000 BC, about 5,000 years ago. It ended in 30 BC, when Rome took over Egypt.

WHY THEY MADE MUMMIES

Egyptians believed they would need their bodies after death. They thought the **soul** would leave the body, then return. Mummification kept the body lifelike. That way the soul could find the body again.

soul: the part of a person that ancient Egyptians believed lived on after death

an Egyptian mummy displayed at the Field Museum in Chicago, Illinois

MAKING A MUMMY

It took 70 days for priests to finish work on a mummy. First they took out the dead person's organs. Then they packed the body with salt to dry it out. When it was dry, priests stuffed the body with rags. Finally, they wrapped the body with long cloth strips.

DISCOVER!

The organs were placed in special jars. The jars were buried with the mummy.

STUDYING MUMMIES

Scientists Richard Evershed and Stephen Buckley studied what kept ancient Egyptian mummies from rotting. They found plant oils and beeswax on the bodies. The scientists believe these items helped keep the bodies protected for thousands of years.

THE FUNERAL

Before burial, priests touched the mummy's mouth with a cutting tool. They believed this act let the person speak and eat after death.

painting in the tomb of Inherka

a mummy in a coffin near its tomb in Saqqara, Egypt

Then the mummy was placed in a coffin. Sometimes one coffin fit inside another.

MUMMY TOMBS

The coffin was sealed inside a **tomb**. The pyramids were tombs for some of Egypt's **pharaohs**. Other kings and important people had simpler tombs. Their tombs were carved into rock. Many tombs are in the hills along the Nile River.

pharaoh: a king in ancient Egypt
tomb: a room for holding a dead body

DISCOVER!

Scientists call one area in Egypt the Valley of the Kings. More than 60 tombs have been found in the valley.

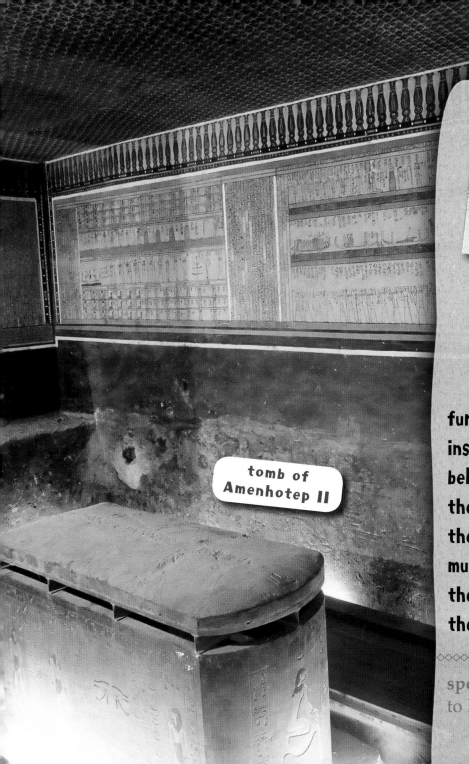

tomb of
Amenhotep II

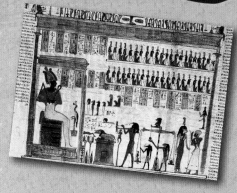

INSIDE THE TOMBS

Scientists have found furniture, weapons, and food inside tombs. The Egyptians believed the soul would need these things. The "Book of the Dead" was also buried with mummies. Egyptians believed these spells would protect the person after death.

spell: words that were believed to have magic power

King Tut

WHO WERE THE MUMMIES?

Most mummies were kings or rich people. Mummification cost a lot of money. Most people could not afford it.

One famous mummy is King Tutankhamun. King Tut's mummy is about 3,300 years old. But even after all that time, his body has not completely rotted.

Seti I and Ramses II were powerful kings in ancient Egypt. Today the kings' mummies rest in a museum in Egypt.

Seti I

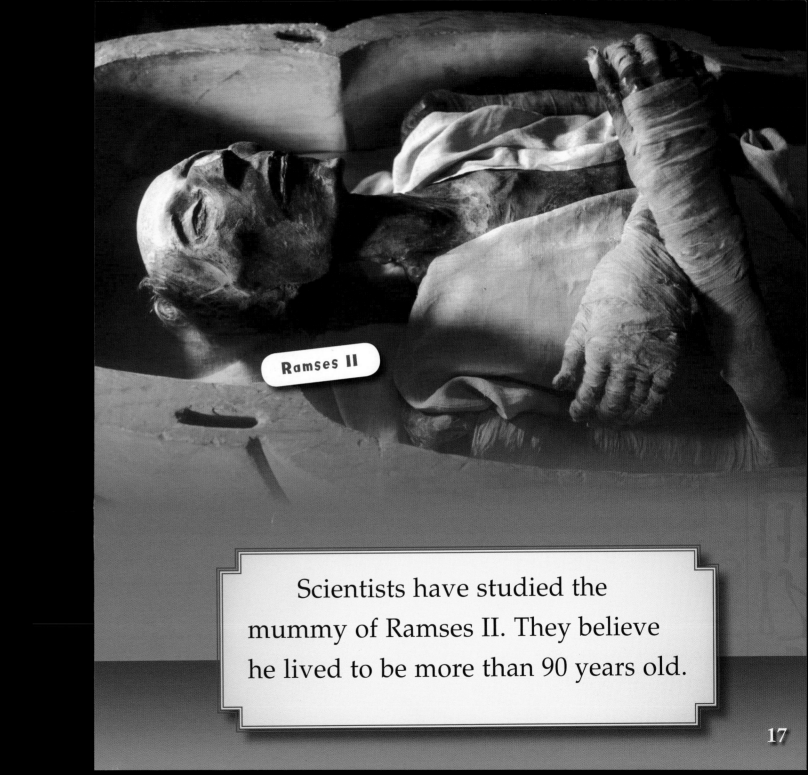

Ramses II

Scientists have studied the mummy of Ramses II. They believe he lived to be more than 90 years old.

Animal Mummies

Egyptians mummified cats, birds, and other animals too. They believed some animals were gods here on earth. Egyptians honored these gods by **preserving** their bodies.

Human or animal, the dead were mummified out of respect. These mummies show people today the world of ancient Egypt.

preserve: to protect

mummified cats

Scientists might have found one of Egypt's most powerful queens. Scientists found a box with Queen Hatshepsut's name on it. Inside the box was a tooth. In 2007, they compared the tooth to two mummies. It fit in only one. Scientists are testing the mummy's body. These tests may prove that she is the queen.

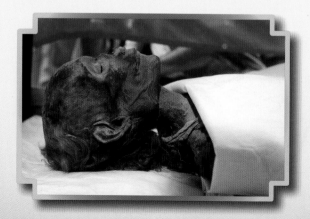

Hands On: Make a Mummy

You can pretend to be an ancient Egyptian. Make a mummy with some things you have around the house.

What You Need

- large lump of modeling clay
- old T-shirt
- scissors
- spoon
- 1 cup of flour
- 2 cups of water
- bowl
- wax paper

What You Do

1. Form the modeling clay into the shape of a human body. Don't worry about details like a face. It's going to be covered up.

2. Cut the T-shirt into thin strips that are long enough to wrap around the clay mummy.

3. Use the spoon to mix the flour and water in the bowl.

4. Soak each cloth strip in the flour mixture. This will help the strips stick together as you wrap.

5. On the wax paper, wrap the clay body tightly in the strips. Start with the head.

6. Let your mummy dry on the wax paper overnight.

Glossary

mummification (muh-mi-fuh-KAY-shun) — the process of making a mummy to preserve a dead person's body

pharaoh (FAIR-oh) — a king in ancient Egypt

preserve (pri-ZURV) — to protect something so that it stays in its original condition

soul (SOLE) — the spiritual part of a person that ancient Egyptians believed lived on after death

spell (SPEL) — a word or words supposed to have magical powers

tomb (TOOM) — a grave, room, or building used to hold a dead body

READ MORE

Fleury, Kevin. *Mummies*. Up Close. New York: PowerKids Press, 2007.

Ganeri, Anita. *Mummies and Ancient Egypt*. A First Look at History. Milwaukee: Gareth Stevens, 2005.

Gibbons, Gail. *Mummies, Pyramids, and Pharaohs: A Book about Ancient Egypt*. New York: Little, Brown, 2004.

INTERNET SITES

FactHound offers a safe, fun way to find Internet sites related to this book. All of the sites on FactHound have been researched by our staff.

Here's how:
1. Visit *www.facthound.com*
2. Choose your grade level.
3. Type in this book ID **1429619163** for age-appropriate sites. You may also browse subjects by clicking on letters, or by clicking on pictures and words.
4. Click on the **Fetch It** button.

FactHound will fetch the best sites for you!

Index